THE Magic OF MOthers

Written and Compiled by Laurie Kay

My grandmother and mother provided the inspiration for this book.
As a young girl, I discovered a shoebox of keepsakes gathered by my
mother. Among the items in the box were pages on which Mom had
written down things she remembered her mother doing for her that
made her feel special as a child. I was touched by what I read and later
in life found her examples to be helpful in raising my own children.

In this book you will find a variety of memories, shared by many.
You will discover that these — and your own inspirational
memories — truly reveal the magic that is... The Magic of Mothers.

This book is dedicated
to my **Mother**

Sometimes when we were home on school vacation Mom had to go to work and couldn't stay home with us. Before she left the house, she set up projects for us to do during the day, such as make a craft, put on a play, or make up a song and dance show. We excitedly worked on our projects all day and proudly presented our creation to her when she came home at the end of the day.

- Scott

I always felt sad when my mother had to

leave on long business trips. To help me feel better

when she was leaving, she *kissed a*

tissue — leaving a lipstick imprint — and

gave it to me to keep as her kiss until she returned.

- Judy

Whenever we had a new baby in the family, my

brothers and sisters and I would gather around and

lean on the arms of the oversized rocking chair to

watch as Mother gently rocked the baby to

sleep. As she rocked, she made up

songs and softly sang them to us. Accepting

our mother's wit, our favorite song of all was,

"Don't Lean on the Chair When I'm Rocking."

- Evanne

On days when I was feeling a little

"under the weather," Mother put

chicken soup in a teapot and we had a

special tea party.

- Debbie

To comfort me when we were apart,
my mother sprayed *her favorite*
perfume onto a white cotton glove

and gave it to me so I would feel

close to her until she returned.

- Nomi

As a small child, sometimes I was afraid to go to bed at night. To soothe my fears, my mother placed her shoes a few inches apart on the floor by my bed. Then she lovingly placed my two small shoes between them. With my shoes *carefully tucked* between hers, I felt safe and was able to go to sleep.

- Rosanne

To make housecleaning fun for the eight children in

our family, Mother *played*

marching music and we

marched from one room of the house to another,

happily picking up toys and putting them away.

- Laurie

When I went to youth summer camp, I happily discovered special *notes of love* and encouragement that my mother had hidden in my luggage.

- Joseph

As a young child I was very frightened by thunder and lightning storms. During these storms Mother wrapped me in a blanket and we snuggled in the rocking chair *sipping hot chocolate* until the storm ended. (Today I am a college student studying meteorology and severe storms.)

- Tiffany

*M*other was always doing things to reach out and

help others in any way she could. Instead of just

doing these things herself, she involved my brothers

and sisters and I in these efforts. As a result, we

learned at a very early age the special feeling that

comes with helping others.

- Val

No matter what, my mother always said,

"I love you" every time

I left the house. I felt secure in her

commitment of love for me.

- Jeff

When I was five years old, I suffered a severe illness

for several months. During this difficult time,

I saw the compassionate

side of my seemingly stern mother as she

spent many hours soothing and comforting me

by softly stroking my cheeks — the only place

on my body that didn't hurt.

- Larry

My **mother's** *laughter*

could always be heard ringing throughout the house.

Hearing it always made everyone feel happy.

- Craig

No matter what she was doing,

how busy she was, or what was going on

in her world, Mother always took

time to listen.

- Lois

Mother was always very generous in showing me

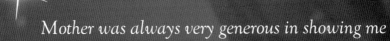

her appreciation for the

things I did and it made me feel good.

- Ed

When I was about age four, I was very, very ill

for many days. In the middle of one of those

long nights, I woke up and saw my exhausted

mother asleep at the bottom of my bed — still dressed in the

clothes she had on that day.

- Anonymous

Just for fun, or as a reward for being especially good, Mom would play a game with me. On little pieces of paper, she wrote messages containing clues and hid them throughout the house. By finding the notes and following the clues, I was led on a hunt to discover a small treasure she had hidden for me.

- Tiffany

Even though she had eight children, Mother

had the ability to make each of us feel

individually loved

in her special way and never showed favoritism

for one child over another.

- Don

As a child, I was always finding things to bring to show Mom. No matter how silly or unimportant it may have seemed or how busy she was, she always stopped whatever she was doing, bent down to look at it appreciatively, and then exclaimed, "Oh boy!" Her actions meant so much to me that now, as a father, I do the same with my daughter.

- Tim

Whenever I was sick, Mom sat and held me for a

long time. To this day when I am not feeling well,

I call Mom. Just *hearing her*

voice makes me feel better.

- Kara

When I needed to calm down, Mother would lightly tickle my hands and feet, which *relaxed and soothed me.*

- Gene

My mom *never failed to notice* when I was in dire straits. Even if I didn't let on, she could always tell if I was sick, tired or upset and would spend time with me until I felt better. I treasured her ability to be so tuned-in and take time to be with me.

- Perrins

When I was unhappy, having a rough day, had a

special performance at school, or was traveling

away from home, Mother *boosted*

my spirits by writing me notes of

encouragement and love.

- Janice

Every summer Mom planned a few days of *special vacation time* with my brothers and sisters and me. These vacations were never very fancy, but we loved her tradition of just spending family time together in this way.

- Christina

My mother always made me feel special

because she gave me lots of

hugs and kisses.

- Mara

We *felt special* when Mom made up a song with our names in it for me and each of my brothers and sisters.

- Deborah

On Friday nights, my friends would come over

to my house and we listened to Mom *read*

stories. This was so special that even

as a teenager, this became my favorite way

to spend Friday night!

- Caleb

*O*nce, I was moved to tears while watching a muscular dystrophy telethon. My mother consoled me and suggested I consider a career in helping physically challenged children. This episode with my mother inspired me and now I have a wonderful career as a pediatric physical therapist.

- Jacqueline

Mother always guided and supported us in a loving way.

She never punished us unfairly.

- Rosanne

Even in the face of adversity,

Mom was always upbeat and had a smile

on her face. She made *everything*

seem okay for all of us.

- Robin

I felt comforted when my

mother lovingly rubbed my cheeks and lightly

rubbed medication on my chest when I was sick.

- Greg

Sometimes Mom and I made up songs together

and tape-recorded them for posterity. For many

years, I loved to re-play the tapes, remembering

how much fun
we had when we made them.

- Scott

Whenever Mom baked bread, she gave me a bit of bread dough so I could bake my own small loaf along with her. *Baking together* was a special time for us.

- Rhonda

I rarely saw my mother because she worked two jobs. She would come home, tired, in the middle of the night. But before going to bed, she would fix me a sack lunch to take to school in the morning. Often, I opened my lunch at school and was touched when I found she had caringly written me a note with a *special message* about something that was going on in my life at that time.

- Maria

Sootie, our black cat, always seemed to claim

ownership of my mother's lap as she sat in her easy

chair. Whenever my mother moved Sootie from

her lap to pick me up and hold me, I felt

very special.

- Sue

Mom always had something good cooking

on the stove. As it simmered, it filled the house

with a smell so wonderful that it had a

calming effect on everyone.

- Nan

My mother used to tell us butterfly stories.
These were ongoing adventures that she
made up about a butterfly. Each time she told
a story, she picked a different child in our family
to be the main character along with the butterfly.
I always felt very special when it was my turn
to be in the story.

- Debbie

When my stepmother tucked me into bed,

she would lie beside me and we'd look up at the

ceiling and **talk and laugh.**

She really listened to me — showing great interest

in what was going on in my life.

- Ed

Every time we had a new baby in the family,

Mother let me help her take care of my new

brother or sister. This made me *feel*

special and I never felt left out.

- Sarah

Waking up on Saturday mornings was always

a special time for me during my childhood.

My mother had the house warmed up,

the TV tuned to my favorite cartoon, and I could

smell that she had **something good baking** in the oven!

- Mirela

Mom would lay out long sheets of white butcher paper and *encourage me* and my friends to color or paint any kind of picture we wanted! One of my friends who always came over to paint on butcher paper with me is now a professional artist!

- Caleb

Whenever I was sick, Mom *showed her love* and concern by making me a special meal and giving me lots of ginger ale.

- Keiki

While sitting around the table during family birthday celebrations, my mother would *tell* **something special** about the person celebrating their birthday then encouraged others around the table to do the same.

- Hanna

My mother always encouraged me to go to college,

even though I didn't think I was smart enough. Her

encouragement and *unwavering*

faith in me helped me stay in school and

was the best thing I ever did for myself.

- Jim

Sometimes as a *special treat* –
if I had been very good — my mother would let me
have a backwards meal. I always liked a backwards meal because I got to eat my dessert first and
then the rest of my meal!

- Debbie

Often, as part of my birthday parties, Mother would encourage me to plan a production such as a Western movie, fake pie fight, drama, or comedy. My friends and I created the birthday production and acted out all the parts as Mother videotaped it. Afterwards, we delighted in watching our acting antics as she played the movie back for us. It was always the best birthday party in the neighborhood!

- Caleb

In Mom's homemade cherry pies there was often

a hidden cherry seed. She always made it

extra fun to eat the pie because she

gave us a quarter if we found the seed. I always felt

special when I found it!

- David

Mother always said,

"Don't worry, everything will turn out

just the way it's supposed to" — and it did.

- Pat

I got third place in a spelling bee contest

and afterward my mom congratulated me

with a card and one of my *favorite*

cookies. I felt very special!

- Morgan

On days when we couldn't go outside to play, Mom hid a note with a written or picture clue that led us to the next note — repeating this process several times until we found the "hidden treasure."

- Scott

Our family found comfort in *playing cards together.* I remember how special I felt when Mom taught me to play canasta and rummy when I was five!

- Nan

Because we couldn't afford the special character

socks that all the kids were wearing at school, Mom

took me to the craft store and helped me get

everything I needed

to make my own special pair.

- Susan

My mother, who lived to be 103, encouraged me in music. I remember sitting under the ironing board, looking up at the underside of it as she ironed and sang to me. Later in life, even though our family didn't have much money, she *always supported me* and somehow saw that I received instruments and other things that were needed to advance my musical talent. As a result, I have enjoyed a notable career in the world of jazz.

- Bill

On my first day of school I was upset because I didn't want to be away from my mother. As I got dressed for school, Mother put one of her necklaces on me. Wearing *her necklace* helped me feel close to her all day.

- Melissa

If this book has touched you and you would like to share
with us a memory of your own, please email us at
memory@magicof.com

© 2005 Havoc Publishing
San Diego, California
U.S.A.

Text by Laurie Kay

ISBN 0-7416-1321-2

www.havocpub.com

Made in China